THE DEFINITION OF JOY

THE DEFINITION OF JOY

Joy Ladin

The Sheep Meadow Press
Rhinebeck, New York

Designed and typeset by The Sheep Meadow Press
Distributed by The University Press of New England

All inquiries and permission requests should be addressed to the publisher:

The Sheep Meadow Press
PO Box 84
Rhinebeck, NY 12572

Library of Congress Cataloging-in-Publication Data

Ladin, Joy, 1961–
The definition of joy / Joy Ladin.
    p. cm.
ISBN 978-1-937679-05-7
I. Title.
PS3612.A36D44 2012
811'.6--dc23

                                        2012002898

Ever love, ever the sobbing liquid of life.

Walt Whitman
"Song of Myself," section 42

Acknowledgements

Poems in this collection have appeared, sometimes in different versions, in the following publications:

"They Say," "Need to Know" and "Children": Storyscape Journal

"Birthday at the Book Mill," "Sickness and Health," and "You Can't Be Afraid Of The Pain That Is Coming": New Haven Review

"Pronounciation": Drunken Boat

"Disease's Gifts": ANTIthesis

"Everything and Nothing": Sweet

"Lost and Found," "Essence and Flow" and "North and South": EOAGH: A Journal of the Arts

"Breath": Milk and Honey: A Celebration of Jewish Lesbian Poetry. (Ed. Julie Enszer, A Midsummer Night's Press, 2011)

"Good News," "Story and Song," "All of Them are Burning" and "Branching": American Poetry Review

"Sex" and "Kiss": LambdaLiterary.org

This book, as a whole and in many of its parts, has benefited enormously from the insight and care of Stanley Moss.

Contents

I. Branching

II. History

III. Everything and Nothing

IV. On the Line

V. World Enough

VI. The Definition of Joy

I

Branching

for Liz

Proof

You prove the world, this blackened world, is shining and full
of the soul your soul resurrects
from what in me was dead.

Before you, I was a landfill, a pinch of salt,
aluminum clamped
to pouting lips of pain.

You say it isn't you. That's normal:
to you you aren't a champagne trapeze, a republic of light, a small
but blazing tree of life.

When you see yourself, you see sensitivity magnified,
chapped canyons, crowded streets
tangled like veins inside.

I see them too. That's my proof
I'm telling the truth:
before you, I didn't know

I was alive.

Spring Break

Love rampages through me, famous love,
addictive love, contradictory Easter-egg love
blushing and burning, abusing my pulse

with the ravenous embarrassment of being a being
the fever-sun of love
inks with zebras and roses, buffalo and pomegranates.

The body I've babysat since I was born
is breaking open like love-sick lips,
admitting the better, edgier world

vibrating through me, casually reshaping lifetimes of starvation,
melting the voluptuous waste of my face
like a snowbank in the spring

into which, without prior notification,
my broken heart breaks.

Pronounciation

Your body is a word
I'm dying to pronounce, hypnotized by the boy
tensing inside you,

panther-waisted Dutch-sketched equestrian
lounging on horseback,
skin polished ivory, lips coral.

Sun just up, you are – he is –
twisting your torso toward the world,
the true and fictional world

I thread, a true and fictional girl
against a sun-shot wall, vined with desire
to performatively pronounce

myself as whole as you: girl
and boy, alone and smitten, ridden and riding off
on wondrous muscles,

thoughtless and thoughtful as the sky
reflected in the river
I undrink as I return to life

determined to remember
the I I ditched
when I ditched the world,

physical, metaphysical
and wholly true
as you.

Developmental

I swerve and spin,
sphered by the sense
of forever splashing toward us

through waves of hair and lips.
You are here, my here,
my will be, my is,

a devastating communication
of brook and oak, redness,
unity and division,

sexing and starring my mixed-up heavens,
circulating in rings
through the psychology of my skin.

You sink and I sink, summer
and I summer, a crystal breaking
into youth and age, instant and forever.

Time

We curl around each other's salt,
braiding creation and Creation
into a tightly packed coil

from which wisps and waves of time,
multiple and opposite,
are shaken and shaped

to the shining salt of our skin. Time
ends here you say, or is that me, or is here
where time begins,

in our spray, our salt, our nakedness,
in the whole cramped clamp of time
unbraiding like hair along our spines,

teased, tousled, flying.

Sex

After great sex, a formative feeling comes. Bodies part
into body parts, napes and necks
and privates nakedness makes

somehow more private. Souls and fingers
unlace, something unspeakably good
shreds and settles, silvering our skin.

We giggle, plan, get out of bed,
coat ourselves in separateness,
play ourselves in miniature –

I apologizing for no reason, you worrying
you're pushing me away –
sinking together into the depths

of not quite knowing one another,
not quite sure
if the selves we expose are us,

or bubbles on the ocean, the same old ocean,
of circulating skin
that's metamorphosing us

into something new, shoots of boy
spangling stalks of girl
slicked by the strangely formal rain

greening our tangled trunks.

Unparting

Time splits us into separate hours, disparate days, fingers
fingering something other than one another,
and by the time time re-members us,

we're nervous, ruffled, skinned and spined, flirting with feeling harmed
by the memory of how twined we were, and aren't.
I do it well – fur up with hurt, pout for the past whose tense

leathers my parted parts like a lash–
and I can't think of anything cooler to do
than dog your distance,

a midnight whistle, an unpaired shoe, a question
that can't stop asking you, an adolescent lyric of love
doing my best to embarrass us both

by proving true.

Kiss

We meet at the lip
of the hole love digs. Come here
you say, meaning down, meaning in, meaning love

has exposed how naked I am, how worn, how young,
how totally yours, how kittenish.
Is that what made you laugh?

I'm too tired to ask. I dream
of hurting and being hurt, I call my children
but they don't answer, I call my answers, my old answers –

God, karma, trees in flower –
but they don't pick up the phone. The hole
is getting deeper. Does that mean we're getting closer?

That I'm your girl? That I am
a girl, and not just a hole
love is digging

deeper and deeper? Come here you say,
meaning your arms that fit
my need to fit somewhere, meaning

you've been waiting for me
since I was someone you'd never imagined,
meaning the hole

love digs through our differences
which are bigger and not as big
as the differences between fear and laughter, water and air,

between a former lover
sliding a finger between your legs
and my lips dissolving

against your lips, between the lips
of the holes love digs
and the lips my fingers kiss.

Curl

We lived so much before we met:
addictions and tingles, conversations with angels
we're too smart to believe in, adulthoods splashing romantically and
        unromantically

through the crudely falling water of sex.
Even now, we don't complete each other's sentences,
thread one another's needles, needle each other's threads.

We lunch, text, use our teeth in bed,
touch each other in the usual places
with unusual confidence.

You fix my hair and pronunciation,
shop for shirts and Romantic manuscripts,
bike when you can, make my life...

Period. End of sentence.
I give you – I try to –
I fear I have nothing to give

but my aging, disastrous lace
of boy- and girlishness, and the truth
you see in my face,

growing older as I grow younger, teaching me
to brush, to spoon, to have skin, to whisper,
to manage the unmanageable spill of curls

of my love for you.

Branching

Let's talk about the tree, the tree of life,
the life branching before and after
the moment I saw you

that sings, still, on my skin
not like a branch but like a finger, a dry finger,
extracting music from the lip of a glass.

The tree isn't music, isn't glass, its branches aren't your fingers
sliding through my hair, it didn't spring up when we met.
Your childhood nests in its branches, the wildness you remember

stalking your sorrow, tightening bike chains,
animating libraries of alter egos, secret agents and gladiators,
arranging clandestine meetings among the leaves

with the God you found
winding your fear and ecstasy
into the whirlwind of desire

that kites you, still, into arms and branches,
the inescapable branches
of the tree of life.

Circles

We never go to bars, lover, we stroll right past
the bright, damaged signs
designed to attract and reflect

the damaged brightness
of those who haunt the hammered canyons
in which you've grown and outgrown

version after version of desire.
We stroll past trees and singing strangers,
sometimes holding hands, sometimes sliding

finger against finger, sometimes strolling side by side
alone through loneliness, our separate renditions
of the pulpy disappointed houses

that haunt our happiness.
Sometimes we're brand-new animals
holding brand-new hands

and sometimes we're sculpted, shaped and labeled
by the eyes of strangers
who notice I feel sexier with you

than with the cleverest, best-built man —
wait, is he gay too? —
and sometimes the future we're beginning to remember

circles our shoulders, guiding us back
to the moment of Creation
naked and nervous in our bed,

the original wisp of time and space
curled into a sexual breath, the breath in which God said
"Let there be" and "It is good,"

the breath I take when I feel your fingers
scouting my uncreated places, unlocking the strangeness
of our differences,

our little worries and toughened hearts
softening like raspberries
under the hot but hidden sun of love

that promises and shadows so much, glittering
on the Caribbean I become
as you unhalter my skin,

whispering something neither of us will remember
a moment later, when God has taken
our still-untaken breath.

II

History

Mortal Sin

Let's face it: death's sexy
in that bad-news way, all clicking zippers
and drooping lids, sacred circus-whip

smoke-wreathed sneer, one part incense, one part hash,
one part mentholated metaphysics.
Maybe it's his fingers – they burn

as they grab your ass –
maybe his lava lips, smothering
your Pompeii flesh with a hiss,

the lifelike murals into which your life has flattened,
the face and figure flaws
other lovers kiss, stupid enough to settle for less than the perfection

that will write death's name in your ash
whenever he's done kissing
whatever's left to kiss. He makes it hurt

as much as he can, a bully
who needs you
to despise him, desperation

masquerading as apocalypse. Hot but not
such a great sin after all. Just the same old ache
of consciousness

you fuck him to escape,
the same old stench
of exhaustion, disappointment – humanness.

You Can't Be Afraid Of The Pain That Is Coming

The you you can't be
Afraid of is coming
The pain of the you

You can't be
The you that's afraid
The afraid that is you

The can't be that is the pain
Of the you
That is coming

The pain that is you
The can't be that is
The you you can't be

Afraid of is coming

History

1. Furnishing Your Life

You know you're missing something,
some nugget of the truth
you planned to distribute among your children
as you sank beside them into the future
that no longer bubbles inside you
though you still have plenty to keep you going,
plenty of freedom
and plenty of executions
in the small, lazy country of your life
where every day you waste the same exact permission
to make yourself a place
you can bear to live in,
too kicked and combed by hunger for home
to escape from the future
that's swallowed the home
you miss.

2. Escape

Window-shopping, squirreling away, ironizing
yourself into making whatever sense you can
of the loss that's driving you mad, the amputated
but living muscle, bloody, palpable, spent,
of the binding contract
of the love
you plan, even now, to forget.

3. Love

You seem to be falling in love
with the continuously failing fallen world
that spins continuously through your versions
of how and who you are: versions
shot full of derivative ideas, blatantly bad versions
that make you feel tougher, versions you despise
and versions you protect out of loyalty
to their smooth unworldly vanilla, versions that paper over
the sparks and fluids cycling at the center
of the version of you –
is this one true? – that orders you
to violate the fidelity
to small-time thinking
that subjects you to being someone who's neither
a spark nor a fluid, someone who cannot flower or bear
the seed of the world
falling fruitlessly through the versions of you
toward the earth
you aren't.

4. Fluid

Bleeding is normal, necessary, even healthy,
the usual side effect of having a heart
unclotted enough to be
sickened by its history of clotting
to its ulcerated partnership with being,
a heart the artery of love
has finally opened, oxygenating
your suffocated future,
splashing your past with blood.

5. Unclotted

The former you
the heart's gone out of
made a home of shrinking
into the reliability of not being,
of losing the life you meant to save,
of fading ever further away
across a widening range of frequencies
to avoid the life of conscious pain
you feel more and more
as you keep falling
from the noise of being
the being you aren't
into the love
you've gained.

6. The Life You Meant to Save

It may be over, but you still feel it,
the temptation to sacrifice
the most important things
for the sake of a life you don't want to live,
the temptation, that is, of dying
into something worth being –
virtue, community, missions
to do great things, huge things
that would save thousands of lives
you'll never have to live – dying
drags you upward
and love pulls you back
into life's unbroken egg,
where you can grow smaller, freer,
less dying, less dead,
where your history can spill
back into time, your time
into time to stretch,
to become grateful, meaningless, generous,
a pocket, a cookie, a handmade globe,
a spit of land, a gift.

7. Gift

You teach your children
what you've been taught
about the generosity of limitations,
the shortness of life, but also the future
you could only find
when you found life's limits,
not the death you lived
but death itself, the real-you death,
divvying up your assets –
your heart, your savvy, your love of interpretation
and interpretation of love
as whatever fulfills your wish
to be and to give
everything that gives itself to you,
that gave your children to you and you to them
when the lines between you were cut or frozen
and pain guaranteed and growing
and love came roaring back.

Evening Sky

The perfect azure
     of childhood's lie, space
brightening with time, window
     on which an unseen moon
has just begun to shine.

Midtown Meltdown

Nothing binds, nothing bounds, nothing mirrors you:
not the woman in crisp black slacks, not the skin
that wraps your bones, not the evening heat

radiating like the filament
of the old porch bulb
on which you watched moths immolate themselves

in summer's childhood.   Some kid's
crayoned the sycamore boles, spray-painted the grass,
tattoed your innermost secret

onto the crowd
washing you into the downtown-bound tunnel
cut through all the hearts

beating with or beaten by
the not-so-secret secret – is it love, or loss? –
shooting like a jet of water

through waves of strangers' faces.

New England Needlepoint

Something golden rising, something risen gilding
evening-thickened limbs. Cold

setting in. Tomorrow's grass
will crack, killing frost

map the shores
of icy continents,

club-foot winter, limping closer, command
pity for all

it will make us suffer. What fed on light
is disappearing. What feeds on darkness

shoulders closer.

Creationism

Let there be You said
and there were
It was a beautiful day
Causality's clock
hadn't started to tick
but everything was finished:
Every birth every senescence
Dinosaurs munching leaves
Little groups of apes
hesitating in trees
and hominids chipping flints
Adolescents reciting lays and city states
Armageddons and armistices
and messiahs thumb-wrestling for the privilege
of announcing history's end
Cells and souls
meshed like gears
the teeth of life
perfectly fitted
to the grin of death

Lost and Found

Brussels airport, 2008

You arrive in pieces
in the world of lost luggage, the only world
you haven't lost: one skirt,

one shirt, one life
sealed into the ark
God builds from the pieces

of you that survive
along with the luggage
of other lives

lost in the world of loss.

Flowering

Even when nothing flowers,
nothing flowers, there is no beauty
like the beauty of nothing

flowering from the very heart
that no longer wants to
but can't stop beating.

Unmourning

Unmourn, unmourn, unfather, unson.
What you've lost is what you've got,
what you aren't the only mirror

in which you can see you are —
something, a glow on the horizon
or some more intimate flicker,

a match struck
against the forehead of darkness, the glimmer
kindled in the corner of an eye

tilting toward the sun.
There's something beautiful in your burning,
an auburn grandeur in your ashes,

a blaze of grief
in your damp, crushed tresses.
Do you know what to do

with your beauty?   Has anyone taught you
to unfurl your fingers, not the fingers you have
but the fingers you are,

little clenched fist
dangling from the sleeve of being?
You've learned to be quite clever

about losing parents and children,
you've learned to like the click and clatter
of the slivers of self you scatter

as yet another version shatters,
you've become a virtuoso mourner,
cycling through stages of grief

like a high-speed washer – rush
of gallons of icy water, a cough, a silence,
the keen of meshing gears of loss

whirling faster and faster. What's left comes out
crumpled but clean,
sopping and clueless, not wanting

to be or to feel anything
but what trickles from its fibers
naturally. Just you

and the child–like tug
of gravity
pulling water from the heart of water

beating in your sleep, and nothing,
not the tiniest whimper of a clue
about what to do

with your beauty.

III

Everything and Nothing

Everything and Nothing

So hard to be everything right now
and so hard not to be, so hard to be
a circle of skin and time

when outside you there are boots
and stars and oranges
and shimmering, twisted trees

and inside you there is nothing, a void
you have taken and mistaken
for a soul, holding on

in the blazing manyness of morning
to the nothing
that is the one thing

you can't lose, the heart,
in fact, of everything
whose voice, seductive and terrifying,

invites you to surrender
the total loss
that beats inside you like a heart

emptied and filled with the blood
of everything that flows
through your body, through the morning, through the trees.

Lost and Found

You find yourself quite comfortable
in the bony clothes of death,
though you seem to have lost the feeling of,

well, feeling. Light moves through you
easily and eerily, as though life were a window
that was broken when you found it

so you can admire without shame
its fracture-stars
that never set, though you find you get a little lost

when you try to navigate by them
though the complicated waste
of loss and obligation

toward the life that spreads across the sky
when you close your eyes,
the stars, that is, of the foundling self,

aroused and assertive, warmed by the hope
you've lost and found
in the bony clothes of death.

Essence and Flow

You live in the gap
between essence and flow,
neither being nor becoming

the essence that is everywhere,
making love or having sex
with every category of existence. Essence flows

over your head and between your legs
and leaves you high and dry, transformed
into something that can't transform,

a borrowed outfit that doesn't fit
your hunger to join the boys and girls
so lusciously compatible with existence

they can forget for years at a time
the nothingness that licks
the glamorous lips of essence. You hang around –

why? who knows?–
bearing witness to the willing world
from the unfashionable position you've fashioned,

beach through which the essence
you aren't
flows into the sea.

North and South

Don't underestimate your need
to cross the line. Frozen
on the wrong side of your desire

to remake the world
inverted in the mirror
of your otherness,

how can you be true
to the truth of being human,
something that bends

in a universe that doesn't, a messy blend
of guts and spirit, responsibility and shame?
You are only an inch

from the constantly moving
source of life, no matter how passionately
you stuff your body

into the too-tight boxes – male or female, north or south,
poor or rich, white
or some other socially demarcated shade –

you check because you are scared
by the lines that keep you safe
from more complicated combinations

and you know no one will mind
you don't have the guts to tell the truth
as long as you stay

on your side of the line.

Not and Enough

Let's face it: it's not enough
to live and die, to cut off the ugly
pieces of life

and beautify
what's left behind. It's not enough
to insist that you are that or this

as though you can distinguish yourself
from the not-enough world
you spin. It's not enough to be afraid

when fear is the air
you were made to breathe,
to hurt yourself instead of admitting

how little you matter, and how much,
and how hard you find
the love that's all you have – you know it's always been –

to interrupt your tendency to twist
your more-than-enough
into not enough

to live.

Die and Live

You're dead, you're dying, you're going to die,
and as everyone tells you
that makes you more alive

to your dying body's
fall and rise.
Don't be shy. You and your body

are still alive, even if you are living
on the darkened side
of the moon that silvers

your dying eyes. They die,
you die, death tolls
the music of life,

luscious, suggestive and sad
as a prom dress lying in the grass.
Something was here, some arms, some neck,

some sweet confusion of sex
with the love
that's wholly gone and wholly there

as that fabulous couple, life and death,
spin away, arm in arm,
into another dance.

Story and Song

There is a story, there's always a story:
horror, sex, birthday cake, designer clothes,
liquefied gas, liquefied flesh,

a house, a bankruptcy, air to breathe, outrage to emit,
a toxic world,
a home, a cabin, a cut-up apple, a bubble

on your dying father's lips,
the story of a world
you were born to claim, to redeem, to suffer,

a story convincing you to begin
and pointing you toward an end
that moves in time to your heart, your loss, your discovery

that nothing's wrong
with your brain, your urinary tract,
or that something definitely is, that your body has stranded you

in a blank white place
that has no story, no tract, no brain. Only here
where all your stories stop

can you hear them sing.

IV

On the Line

Disease's Gifts

for Peggy Munson

That you must accept
what you cannot prevent. That fear inverts
the meaning of success. That you can be fearless

when fear is all you have.
That fear is all you have.
That you aren't alone in loneliness,

there's a whole world here,
a pregnant, fascinating glimpse,
all stomach and hips,

of the life–creating love
you're finally sick enough to feel.
That that glimpse can't stop you from melting

into the futures you fear
you will and will not have.
That you have, you still have,

everything you need to live:
night, ice, plums, a lap and a laptop, a name, a parent,
whipped cream, gossip, steaming plates

of life and death.
That this is the end of the world.
That you will survive it.

Death

No body, no blunders,
no grand ballets of approximation,
no need to avoid or face the truth

that you are addicted
to the foiled desires
that skin with grief

with your love.

Mr. Pain

It's almost an adventure, lying on the couch
with Mr. Pain and his buddies,
watching old movies, getting to know his friends.

It's something new for you
and it's not like you had other plans.
There's a gap in your diary

between rising above disaster
and lying here studying
Mr. Pain's darkening brows,

humming the musical tones that flow
from his remarkably welcoming, multiplayer soul
where everyone can hurt at once

and still be completely alone.

Good News

Even while your body is dying, your life goes on,
off, then on again, a story
that doesn't feel romantic or even focused on you

the way the beaches you visit in your imagination
aren't romantic or focused
on the plastic palm tree

in your hand. The disease
crawling in and out of your brain
leaving star-shaped scabs

is not about discomfort or debt,
creativity, failure, success,
but your body's unwillingness

to distinguish self from other, death from life, infection
from your unbearable craving
to lose yourself

in the steaming juices
that wash the world
and seep between its thighs.

And the good, the really good news is
that what feels like gradual mutilation
has put you in the ideal position,

beaten by hope, buttered by fear, areolas exposed
to the masterful thumbs
of life.

Date Night

You dig the Earth, but suddenly it seems
you have nothing in common. You can't find anything
in yourself to mingle

with Earth's radiant notes of pine and vanilla.
You won't let Earth's laughter
erase the scars

that have validated your pain so long
you look forward to touching them
in the dark. Earth

won't do that stuff with you,
won't let you break up
the ravenous serenade

Earth sings through the pain in your feet
and the pain in your brain
to the unlived life

you're squeezing between your thighs.

Truth

You're not complete, but you know right off the bat
that what you picture as unforgivably ugly,
like a plastic mustache on a burning beehive,

is just your fair share of shame,
natural but false, a zigzag judgment
that flatters your lust

to cheat yourself of life. The truth,
like a silkworm,
speaks without talking, totally sincere

but not a real conversation-maker,
more like a scent, chocolate or apples,
a glimpse of wet silk in moonlight

or a memory of a ribbon
stolen from a sister
you didn't have. The body

frozen in the mirror with a rare disease
is waiting for someone
to lift the pleats of your life,

to touch the skin below the ice,
to unzip the zippered lips of goodness
steaming like milk inside.

You bristle at the light
that winks in your direction.
Once you were a brain in a void, then a feeling of mutilation,

cold but with a sense of humor,
then literature took you by the hand, absorbing your lengthening
        history of loss
by padding it with meaning.

You say you've kissed that waste goodbye,
but you kiss that waste every day,
cheating on the love

that swept you out of the void
into the blazing turquoise music
of becoming

a girl diving from death into life
into the bright, fatal hands
of the truth that whispers

silkworm innuendoes
on the other side.

All of Them Are Burning

Your present, your future, your path
from one to the other.
It's not a bad thing, really.

What more do you need
than a little skin to cover your heart,
a little heart

to cover your losses, a little loss
to hold you in this place
that may not be a place

but is the only place you stand a chance
of finding a way to live.
You get credit for trying

to live when you never have,
for acting natural
when you are an unnatural act,

an impersonation of a person
you'd like to meet, have dinner with, strip
to some essential, attractive fact,

you get credit for refusing to be ashamed
of the act of imagination
that keeps you down here, rooting in the dark,

hurting yourself
and sometimes laughing
in creation's basement.

One Fierce Hip

of your future
pushes into your life's
badly lit basement

which can only fit
one hope, one desire, and one fierce hip
of the future you've exchanged

for everything
you know how to wish for, love and sex
and the even less likely alternatives

you've given up because they would never fit
that burning hip
that promises and costs so much

you willingly, stupidly give.

Stand

March 23, 2009

Even if you don't stand a chance
of touching the face
of love again, you're strong enough to stand here

asking what matters
in the midnight of your life, exploring
your unhealthy body, the awful need

that makes you real, the sun-kissed ugliness
of your becoming.
It's time to make a stand, heartbroken

or not, for the happiness you fear.
You've gotten older, you can stand
looking in the mirror

that's seen so many monsters
when it looks in your direction.
You are, after all, the mirror's daughter,

a powerful expression of the power of impressions,
a lyric process of self-creation
crying and clutching a purse to your stomach,

determined to stand
for a truth that shines
between body and mind

like a drop of milk
on a nipple made of moonlight. It's okay to hide
your difference from the world,

but your difference from yourself
is where you make your stand:
your temple, your truth, your lover's voice

calling you to bed.

Later

It's late, you think, to be seen
as someone to scream over,
a blonde devil, a fatal angel, a merry little Christmas.

You wish you could squeeze
a few more years
of puberty into adulthood, a few more days

when it isn't too late
to learn to navigate
the crash and crush

of becoming. You take a swipe
at a touch of blood
in the mirror, but the blood isn't going away,

it's pulsing in your temples,
asking who you are to jilt the life
waiting like a kiss so right

it doesn't matter
if it means forever
or good night.

On the Line

March 24, 2009

False lines wrapped you in metal, midnight, velvet and ice.
They protected you, they were you,
but now they are over, the you they protected is over,

the tight tornado of the you they were
has bled from the center of your lips
into a smoky blush and a touch of pain

in your eyes. Look, one shoulder, one arm
are pushing forward, single but ready
to be paired, to mingle your dream of being

with the secrets and screws of the life
that's traveling toward you, daring you
to be fearless, to pick matching socks,

to mesh your love-starved intelligence
with the radiant, liquid line
that glows in the creases of your life.

You were born torn, detached, an accident funneled into a skull
the radiant line circles and gathers just in time
for you to have an actual birth,

to be born for a few hours, maybe a day,
maybe the rest of your life, into the world you wished
would burn you away.

Until today.

One Girl

for Liz

can change your life. Suddenly
you are an animal child,
in a body that takes you by surprise

after years of being terrified, citizen
of a secret winter, too frozen to follow
the fragrance of longing

you knew would end your life. You felt so safe,
so grown up, so gagged, trustworthy as an old pillow-case,
an essential, slightly unpleasant routine

marooned in a family chalice. Now you tongue
the butter of hunger, ravenous
for the love you were born to remember,

for the voluptuous innocence of the power
your body unexpectedly radiates, responding
to the mingled perfumes of the earth

that confirm your entry
into the odd perfection of nature.
Now you are far out on the water,

in a full-bodied universe that doesn't care
why or what you are, floating in the arms
of a girl whose kiss

inverts the gravity that kept you staring into the mirror,
a girl who reaches back
through the lacquer of adult pain and fear,

who teases and unzips
the skin you thought would never shed
with a touch you inhale like air

as she runs her fine undarkening fingers
through the fine dark spray
of your hair.

V

World Enough

RIP Dude

JL, 1961-2007

RIP dude, peace to the dead
beard I balded, to your sweaty t-shirts and unclean jeans,
your single-minded devotion to "other people"

because you felt too other
to be a person — dude, you were,
that's why you're dead, why you finally — RIP —

gave up the pretense of being the ghost
in whose lap your kids — now mine — squirmed the language
of their love for you, buttocks muttering of and to

the love that clothed your muscles in skin
you'd have shucked in an instant
if you'd known how to hold them without lap or lips

to press into shampoo-honeyed heads,
no R, no I, no P,
in your unquiet tomb of flesh

jabbed by the elbows and knees of kids
who still can't let you rest;
that's where I come in, offing you every day, teaching you to relax

into oblivion, the only one who knew you
too well to love you, and loves you too well —
dude, I do, too well to pretend

your beard was more than a hairy mask,
your torso more than a skin-wrapped rack
on which to stretch those sweaty shirts, or, at the best of times —

they were your very best — a place for the squirming
flesh of your flesh
to rest — RIP dude — sleepy, shampooed heads.

My Father's Art

Under the finger of his flame, iron blushes
and bends to his will to shape
matter into a man
striding toward the iron blank
he and I will someday make
of what, for one acetylene hour, is love.

He hands me goggles. By the light of burning gas,
I eye the black hairs
rising from and arcing back
to the child-white flesh of his neck,
an image of futility – his –
suffused with tenderness. My father

doesn't hate me yet. Not with iron
bending in his hands, not with nails
becoming arms and legs
walking away from the life
neither he nor I can stand. He teaches me
to point the torch, to steady

the flame of creation
that welds us, for an hour, together,
the image of a son
to the image of the father
I love and fear, as the man of iron must
the man who makes him.

Blind Isaac Blesses

for G

"The smell of my son is like the smell of fields the
Lord has blessed"

My son is a land the Lord has blessed
Unshaven borders frame his face
Unploughed fields dazzled with dew and spiderweb

My son is a blessing
the Lord takes and gives
Once he smelled like fresh-baked bread

Once his head fit in my hand
Now blessed by the Fear I love
he smells of wilderness

This Morning

for Yael

Last night you wanted to kill me.
This morning you're tender, counting down the minutes
we have left together.

The sky of rage, the sky of love,
melt into one another, grow deeper, bluer,
as you lean back against my shoulder.

Mischief ripples across your face,
I feel your sleep-soaked body wake,
a mare gathering her legs beneath her

before she gallops away.

Wake

Light from somewhere – I must be somewhere – pain
tingling in distant limbs, circulating through a system
I can't name – names haven't come back.

Another, better body
yawns and stretches
inside the body I actually have.

Whistles along
with the birds of dawn
I will be I will be I am.

The Bird that Sings at Three AM

The bird that sings at three am
doesn't seem to mind
that his is the only voice

in the dead of the night he serenades
with the self-delighting honesty
of a fact that's true

without meaning to be. He's alone in the tree,
alone on the street, alone in his music
that isn't really music, a few notes, a chuckle and a screech

that accuses and forgives
everything equally: the branch he grips, the reddening leaves,
the sleepers and the sleepless,

burrowed and bedded, rooted and routed, blown and blossoming.

Outside the Pioneer Valley Performing Arts School

The October hills have burned to embers, flaring here and there
where sun kindles leaves
that haven't finished falling.
Brown, muscular beauty, like muscles bunched
in a strenuously dreaming body.

High school students, reluctant to turn from one another,
shuffle toward waiting parents. Mine
doesn't notice me gazing past him
through the windshield of middle-age
that turns October's fading reds and greens

into shades of a single color, the color of time
when its river has frozen
solid enough to support the weight
of a kneeling body
staring through the ice.

Birthday at the Book Mill

August 16, 2010

The drizzly evening light's
just bright enough to see

summer's pages yellowing at the edges
of field and forest. We interrupt our reading to eat

udon noodles, red cabbage shreds, scallion rings.
Time today

is a kind of breath, filling our lungs
the way books fill

the low-ceilinged rooms
of the decades-dead mill. The old women

we will be
skir like the crickets in the grass

murmuring August's psalm. Rock can't reverse
the river's rush, but here and there,

time's whitening hair
blackens in granite's palm.

Rosh Hashanah

The new year begins, the honey-dipped drip
of time against lips
sweetens the abyss
between body and head, between the stoops

where women smoke the night away, strollered babies
dozing to their voices,
and the knife that slices
the apple you dip

into thick white honey. Somewhere bees
busy time's hives, somewhere the pollen
of what blossoms and dies
thickens and sweetens the combs of time,

somewhere – here – fingertips – mine –
comb a lock back from your ear, dip –
five stories down, a baby starts to cry –
crescents cut from the apple of love

into white untasted years.

Old Deerfield Graveyard

We cross the ramshackle fence
that separates, without much fuss – lawn here, lawn there –
the fragility of the living

from the fragility of death: head-
and foot-stones scratched, cracked, pitched and thinned
by centuries of water and wind. Griefs

that were built to last – names and dates,
filial bonds and wedding bands, angels' radiant grimaces –
fade like breath on glass. We bend to decipher

loss' alphabet: you find Mercy, I her daughter, Submit.
Head- and foot-stones
separated by a single stride: an infant. Leaves and branches

bloom on her granite
under stunned inhuman eyes, an angel outraged
by the blossoming God

to whom he testifies. Love,
I'm dizzy again. Submit –
her scoured stones slant, drops

of frozen rain.
The sun is gone. A finger of wind
beckons from the mountain.

Sickness and Health

You wish you could cure me. We float together
in your bed, on a postage-stamp sea
frozen into wood – your charming, warped floor –

that shakes and heaves while you sleep, arm wrapped around my waist
as though you could anchor me,
as though love meant simply holding on,

as though insomnia were simply wrong
when it whispers that we're drifting apart.
Car horn. Hours till dawn. Our bodies

will be here when it comes,
glowing like communion wafers, touching symbols that aren't ours
of the crumbling body – this we share – of God.

I need to say this now
when your arm around my waist
is the only answer you can make

to the heaving sea of boards
which, you'd whisper, if you were awake,
neither shake, nor heave, nor carry me away

because beyond our love there is no sea.
I wish it were true.
That the sea were wood, the wood still tree.

That your love could cure me.

Some Part of Me

Some part of me keeps talking to you
even when we hardly talk

as though I were still horizoned by your arms,
saying I don't know what

when horizon is all we are,
some little cupid's-bow of soul

still whispers to some distant fold of heart,
some lips I didn't know I had

that part when we're apart.

Listening Through Rain

Kampala, December 29, 2010

A rooster crows, a baby screams, a woman "An-drew!"'s over and over,
a young man polishes rain-polished cars, the rooster o – O – O!s as though
there's something he desperately wants us to know,
the scrape of shovel on stone, the muezzin's muffled summons,
gong of drops on a pot, rain on tin, radio throb
of bass and talking drum, slap to pluck, palm to thumb,
unanswered "An-drew!" to rooster crow,
meaningless and meaning.

Joking About Genocide

In Africa. On New Year's eve. "...Rwanda." Big laugh.
At the church across the street, they dance the year to death.
Outside the half-open sliding-glass door, the maid scrubs something
        on the flags.
She won't be done for hours;
not long after dawn, she'll be eggs for breakfast.

The maid lays out our dinner,
Ugandan beans over mashed banana, plain and sweet
as the smiles that sometimes break
through the skins – clingier than class, bonier than convention –
that keep us in our places, waiting and waited on.

So many skins, so many places, so many jokes
we're free to make because no one's killing
here at this table, where one of us serves the three who eat
in the oddly cozy space
between irony and massacre.

The maid – is she out of her teens? – starts clearing.
"Why don't they resist? They'll die one way or the other"
wonders the community college music teacher –
he wrote a book on Wagner –
about refugees awaiting slaughter.

The maid, as usual, avoids our eyes.
The night is full of bodies
shaking – dancing, I mean –
as the year dies
one way or another.

Sick in Kampala

January 3, 2011

Sun-warmed pineapple and hot black coffee. The balcony cool
in the early morning, a bit too cool, in fact.
Two men in dusty workman's clothes
holding hands and laughing, confident
no one will fatally mistake their friendship for love.

Sick so long, sickness becomes a kind of astrology,
a future written in the wheeling houses
of the body I blacken
with another swallow of coffee. It will be night in me
until I touch your body.

You're hidden behind the bulge of the world, sleeping, probably,
and yet I feel you listening through me
to the honk of hornbills, clang of iron hammers,
cries of babies I can't pick up, little murmurs of pain I make
sipping too-hot coffee, murmurs I feel you understand,

as though illness were a sky we share,
a continent to explore,
a balcony.

An Ocean or Two Away

Kampala, January 3, 2011

Palms sway above burnt red roofs, green fronds telling
rosaries of breeze. Police cadets in undershirts

sweat in the middle of the unpaved lane. An ocean or two away,
you're asleep, curled five stories above frozen street.

What I see now – cursive loops of electrified barbed wire,
tires tossed on a battered tin roof, green balls ripening near
        the teetering top

of a jackfruit tree – you will never see.
The continent-spanning structure of our love –

I can almost make it out
among the half-finished frames that crowd

the sky of this rising city, girders scaffolded by handcut poles,
innumerable rooms

open to whatever falls or blows,
no ceilings, no floors, no walls.

Last Day in Uganda

So much here that would hurt your ears. Today
it's the drill, yesterday the blowtorch and the hammers
as the house next door is gutted.

I imagine sinking into your bath – no bath for weeks –
spooning your soup, palming your pears.
You won't know what to say:

you'll blush, I'll stare, we'll look away, your fingers
twitch toward mine, twine and untwine.
I'll stretch out on your bed, close my eyes and listen to you clear

another deliciously awkward dinner,
trying to untangle here from there, together from alone, ache from
        the benediction –
you turn the faucet on – of your skin pouring over mine.

Coming Home

January 8, 2011

The airport check-in line stretches a hundred yards out the door
into African night. Families press against the glass, waving
to children on the other side. A girl of five
pushes baggage heaped to twice her height.
The airport goes black. Twice.

Ten p.m – you're probably cramming lunch
between work and errands. By the time your sun goes down,
I'll be sitting above the clouds, the distance between us thinning
from hemisphere to ocean to the sweeping second-hand
of the impalpable clock of love – of soul – of whatever it is

that synchronizes your time with mine. South of Greenland
now, skimming a sea of sun-splashed cloud,
trying to remember how to pronounce
the syllables of your body.
I live the same minutes over and over – doze, wake, ask for water

as the same dawn breaks across changing skies,
giving me back the hours I lost when I left you behind.
The hands on our clocks slide closer
at hundreds of miles per hour. Later – soon – I won't remember
my fear of crossing

the last dividing line.

Enough

Home again, winter again, outlets designed to power my phone
in a country I call mine: my power, my weather,
my unfriendly immigration officer, my color-coded class system.
You're a terminal away, moving closer,

and then you're here, quizzically returning
my blurted love, hoisting my heaviest bag,
leading me out of the plastic airport haze
in which anywhere is a flight away

into the grounded world of elevated trains
clattering past places you've lived,
places you bicycled with former lovers,
places – a few – you and I have been,

and now I'm letting go of your hand, telling you to read,
feeling the world bulge between us again,
not the simple physical world
that briefly turned my winter to summer

but the private palindromic world
of fear and recognition,
recognition of our fear and fear of our recognition
that even when together we're alone

stretching toward the other
we can neither reach nor abandon.
Fear we recognize as love
we fear will expand and narrow our lives

to a single word: enough.

Snowed In

By the time I make it down to the street, storm has given way
to anthropomorphic heaps, sun-glazed breasts and knees,
snow-layered cars like wedges of wedding cake.
So many weddings and unweddings:
melting into you, pulling away, freezing
into separate shining bodies
slipping and sliding between shadow and light,
shoulders of snow, hips, thighs,
disheveled blankets. Paradise.

VI

The Definition of Joy

All words in this sequence were taken from the online Oxford English Dictionary definition of "joy." The sentences are my own.

Sailor in a Desert

Others are singing, carried along
by the booming gossip
of saints and aeroplanes.

I'm sore; they're laughing.
I'm a sailor in a desert,
falling down and occasionally dying.

They're telling jokes
about God and the world
he ain't been to in years.

I accelerate, a wheeling dimension
on a train that isn't moving,
circling from death to death, tragedy

to the being blow-out
that blows the people I wish I were
into the grief-smoke of becoming.

They sniff the grief
and invite me to supper,
night-grapes, bliss-cake, lemon lament.

I wish I could hear the response
the hot horse pivoting under my skin
keeps singing.

God

Drink fire, says God. It makes sense:
Drinking, fire, God
would trouble my trouble

with establishing any desire
other than desire
for death. Death,

I know, is obsolete,
as is my grief, and my belief
that death will lead me through it

to a spot,
my own small spot,
on the padded midriff of peace.

Drink fire, says God. Easy for God to say
when God is the trouble I drink, the grief that tongues me,
the death that's obsolete.

Envy

Occasionally, I express
God's envy of the world
that dreams, laughs, is amused and drugged, pious

and popping grapes, bereft of peace or means to move
the dead cold stone of lament.
Occasionally, God expresses

my envy of the world I eye
like a small ironic planet.
Occasionally I play with God

for the world we've deserted. The cards
are years: years I've blown,
years I've burned,

years God envies
and with both hands takes
as I make my move.

Two-Dimensional Image

God should elevate
my derelict amusement park of grief,
but I'm not elevating.

My joy-bells aren't ringing,
My joy-pop only pops on occasion, light
only occasionally enlightens

the two-dimensional image
easing along the screen, a plank representing
the strictly horizontal structure I follow

from the little epiphanies of grief
to the love that could free me
from littleness and grief.

Love blunders into me, a wish
that had no intention of coming true.
I still can't believe it has.

I've blundered into love's open hand,
the world of horses, bowls, hippodromes,
hot, troubling desires to couple myself

to the dance I've deflected
into a grand ballet of lament.
Love rings me, wrings me, rings

the bells of wine and awe
ringing in and through
the life, the only life,

love could blunder into.

Ringing

Celebratory shots. Peals of light. Gigantic wheels
encompassing God, encompassing grief,
encompassing my dried-up oscillation

between death and life. Hands
lift me up, into the blaze
I thought I could avoid

by being damned or dead. I am
damned or dead. So?
The time I couldn't tell

is telling me, booming the news that isn't news
now that I know I always knew
that God, my God, who lifts me up,

will never let me go.

The Time I Couldn't Tell

Horizonless, I followed the path I fashioned
from drying springs and dried-up kisses,
irony, ice, the collateral waste of God's happiness.

I was the waste, unblissed, unblessed,
I was the life I deathed
by running after myself, after the misery of having a self,

after the grief-ravished wonder of the self
that obscured the gate — no, it was the gate —
to joy.

God and death and life — no need to make distinctions —
dance in a ring on the other side
where I am dancing too,

coupled and uncoupled, passed from hand to hand,
a conclusion, a completely natural conclusion,
to a love that has no end.

Praise for Joy Ladin

Ladin draws the reader into a world of harsh truths, uncanny beauty, inspired erudition, ironic wit, and cadenced music . . . imagination rules, wedding poetic forms to unflinching meditations on human suffering, terror, love, and unbearable loss. Despite the ubiquity of evil and death in her poems, there is, in Yeats' words, "a gaiety transfiguring all that dread."

–Herb Leibowitz on *The Book of Anna*

Joy Ladin is a devotional poet who is also blasphemous, sometimes simultaneously. What she most surely opposes is cant. The "alternatives to history" that she examines–more accurately, celebrates–have to do with God, ethics, Kabbalah, current events, happiness, and absolution. Her poetry offers a personal view of the big truths. Readers will find, having finished this extraordinary first book, that Ladin has explained what we did not know that we did now know. The fact is, through her poetry Ladin does the reader a favor, a great courtesy. She makes our lives more valuable.

–Stanley Moss on *Alternatives to History*